Wonders
of the World
color by
numbers

Wonders
of the World
color by
numbers

SIRIUS

SIRIUS

This edition published in 2024 by Sirius Publishing, a division of
Arcturus Publishing Limited,
26/27 Bickels Yard, 151–153 Bermondsey Street,
London SE1 3HA

ISBN: 978-1-3988-3633-4
CH011384NT

Printed in China

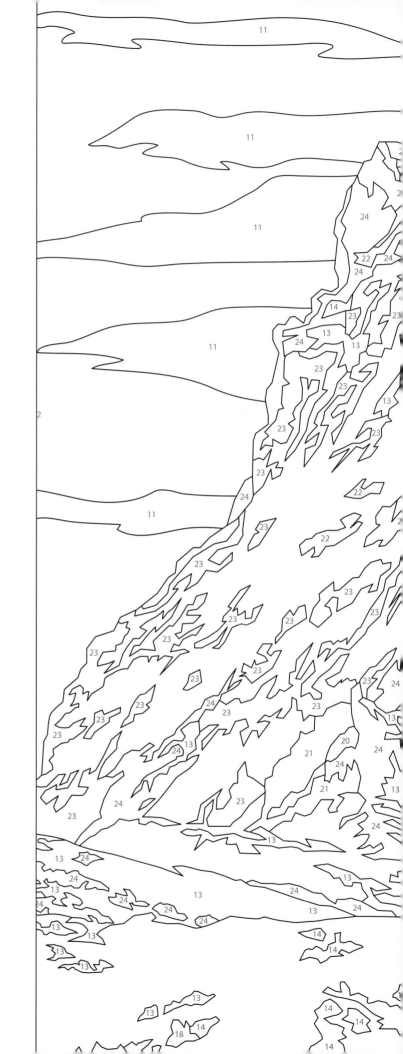

Introduction

Take a whirlwind journey of the world's greatest wonders from the comfort of your home with this selection of color-by-number images. When in need of a break from the stress and bustle of day-to-day life, simply pick up your pencils and visit the stunning Statue of Liberty in New York City. Or perhaps flit off to Sydney to get a glimpse of the glorious architecture of the Sydney Opera House.

Each image is fully numbered so that you can build up an accomplished final image. Using the color key on the inside cover, match your set of colored pencils to the colors in the key. If there is no number, the space should be left white or colored with a white pencil. Take your time to match your pencils and slowly build up the color within the image. While some of the more complex images will require patience and concentration to complete, you will be rewarded as one of the world's great wonders begins to take shape.

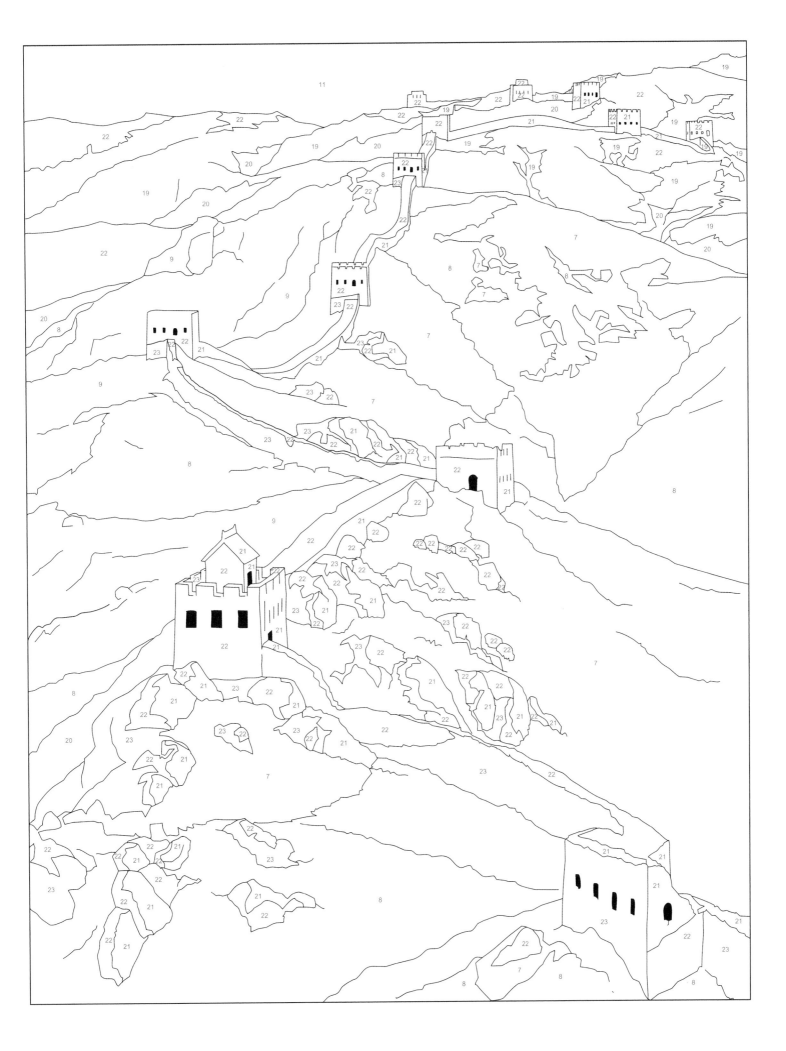

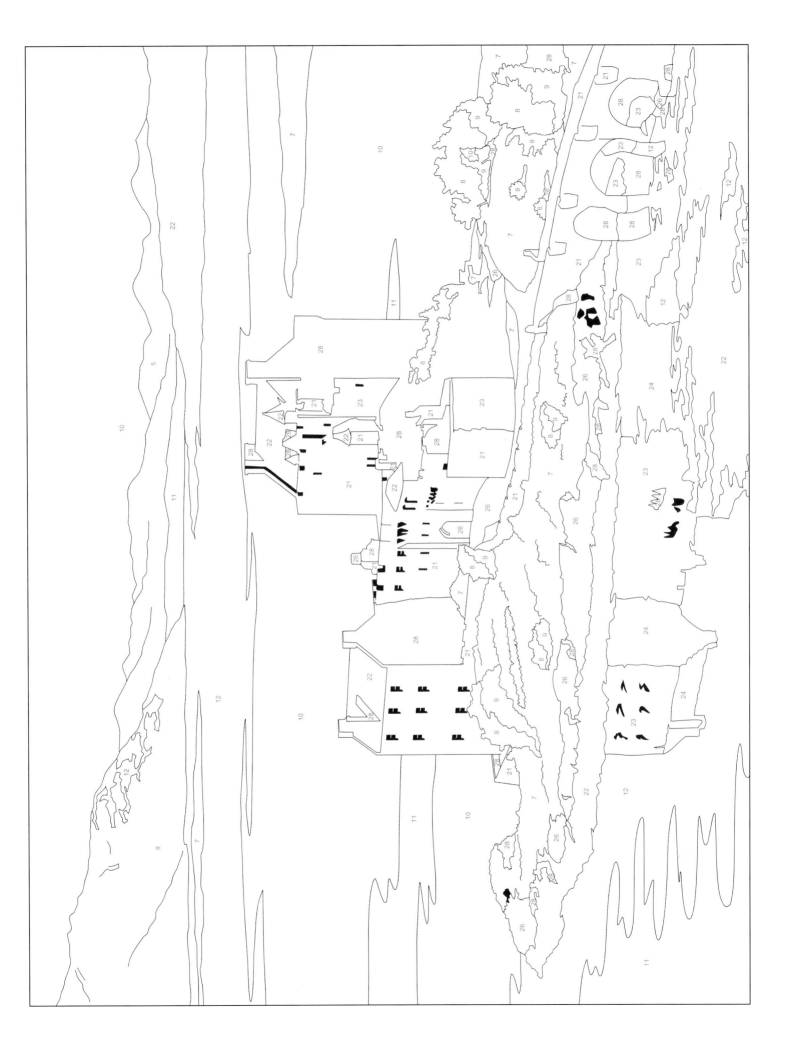

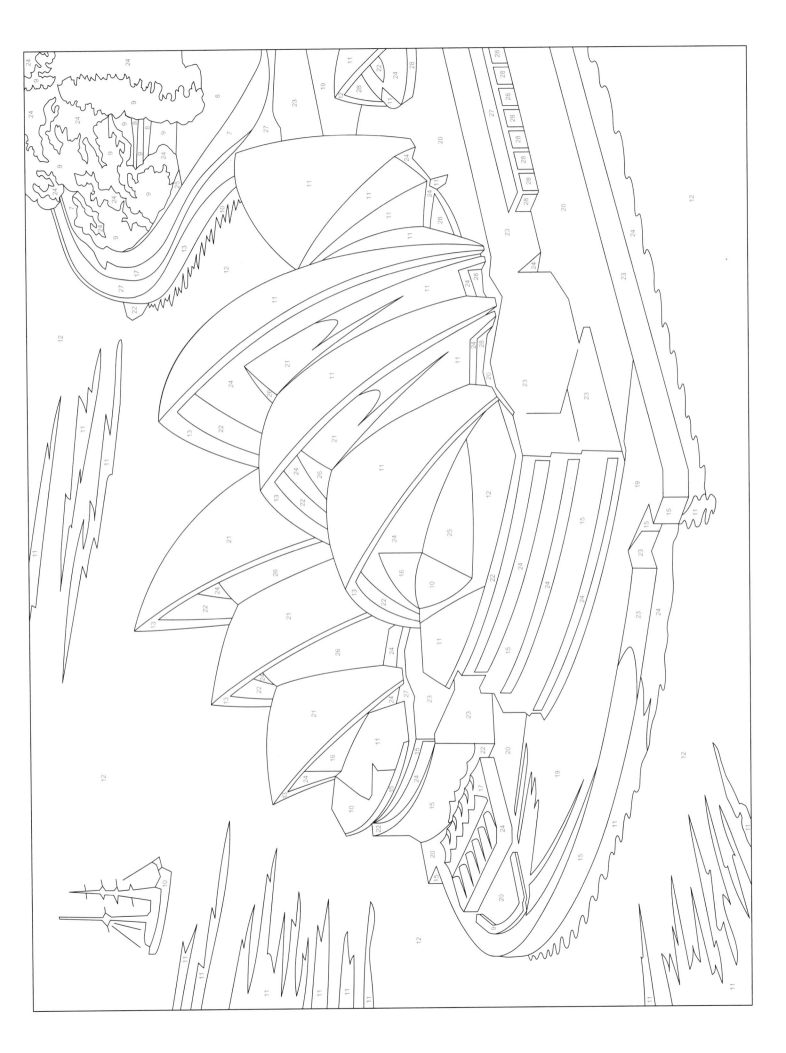

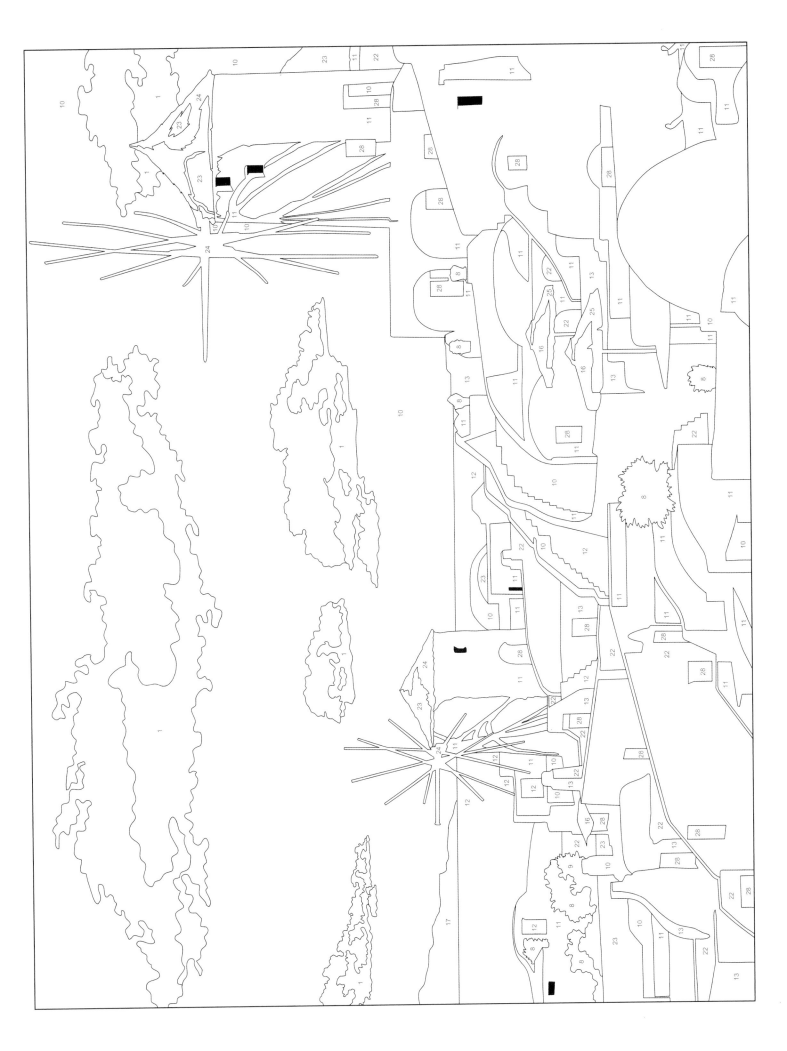

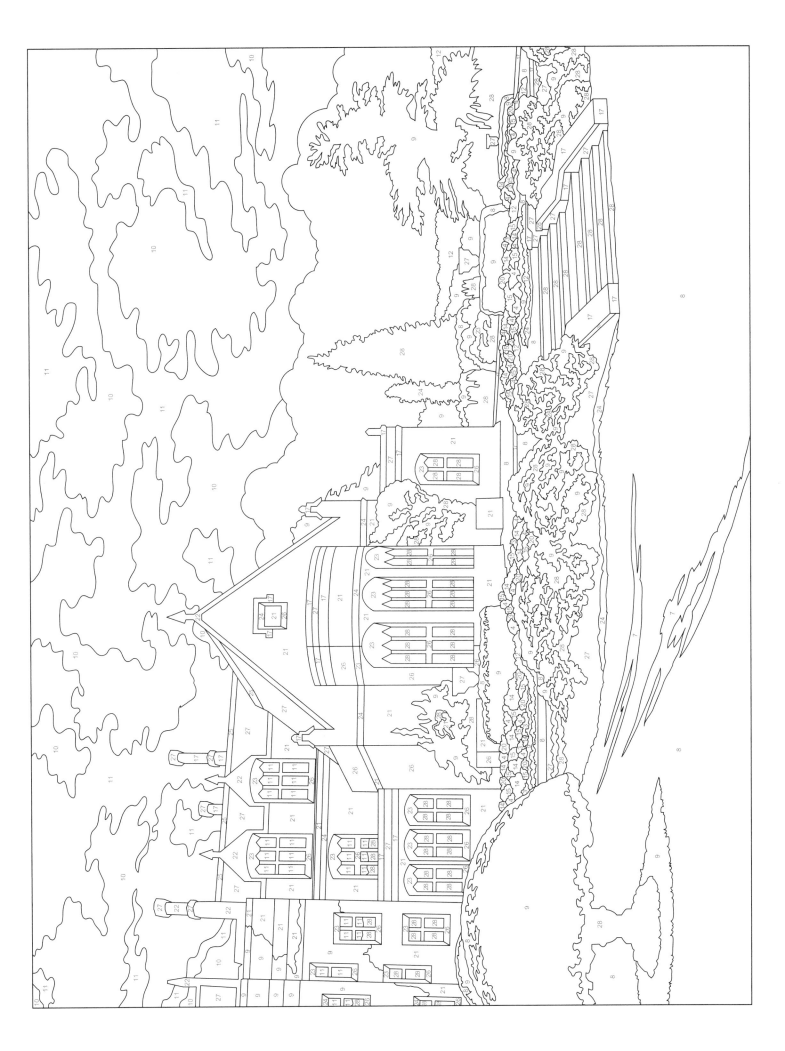

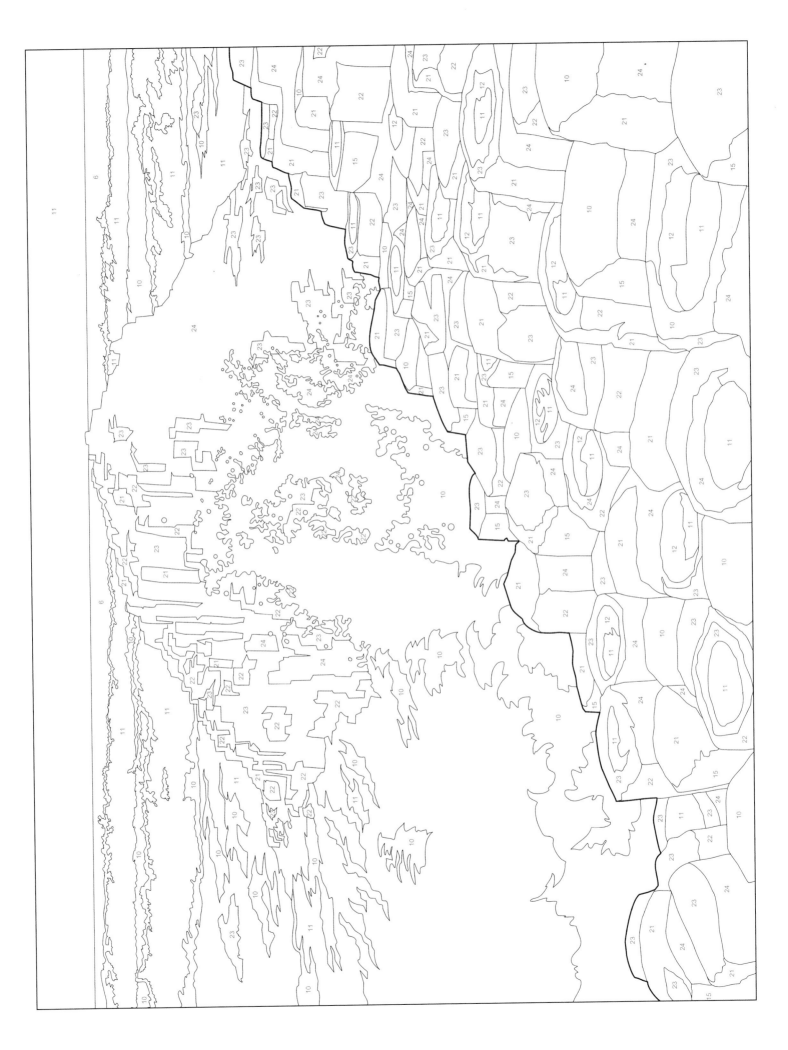

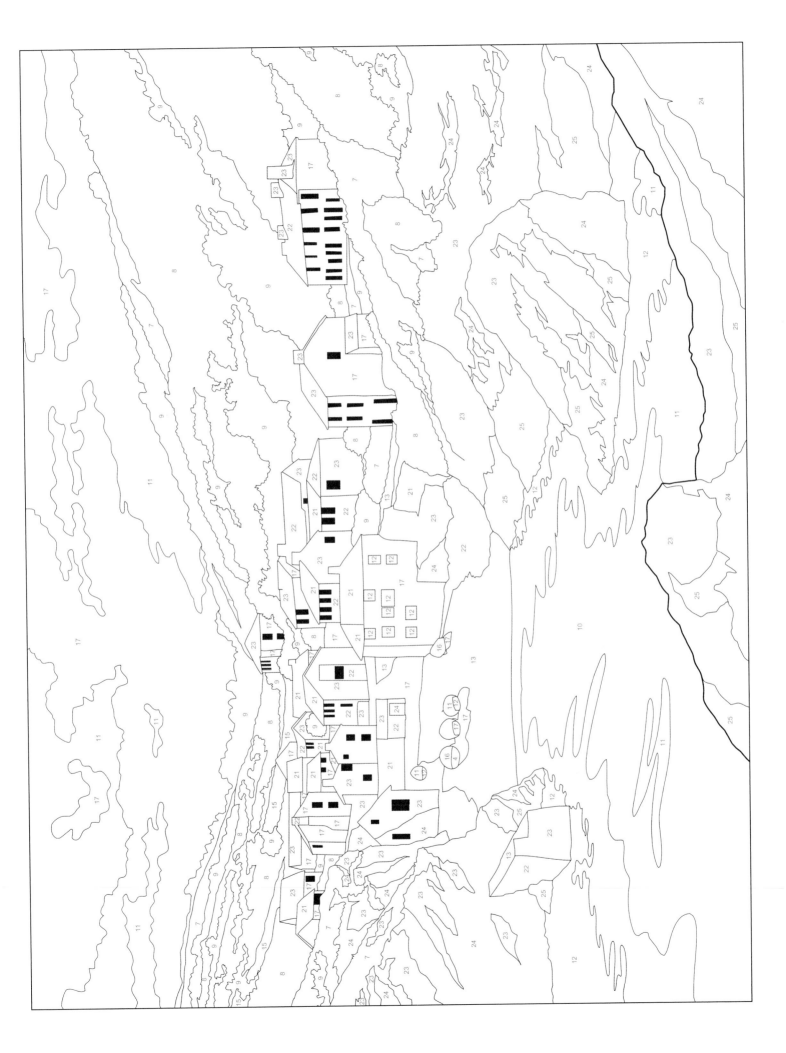

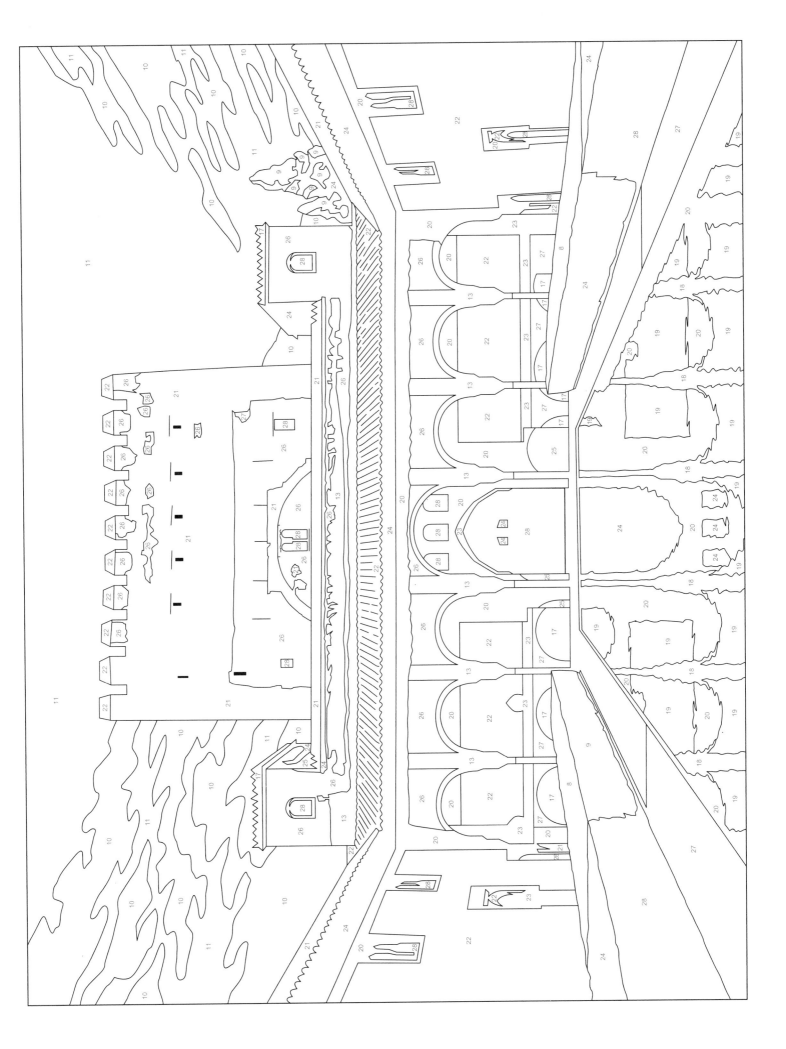

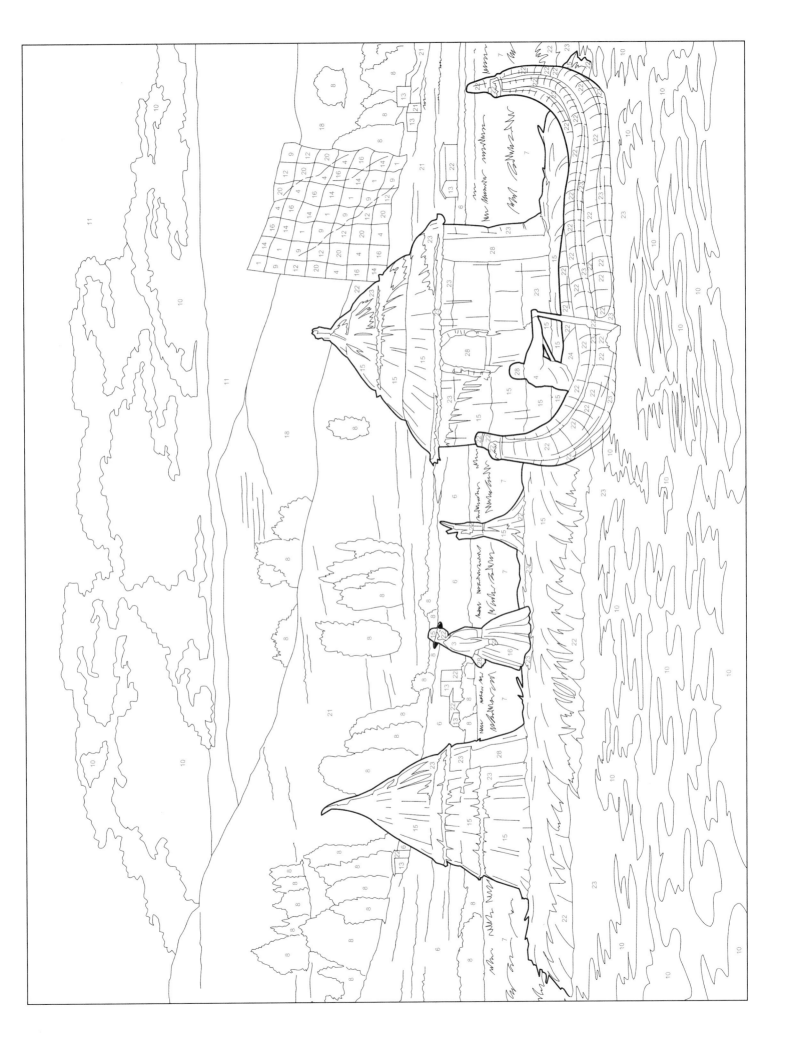

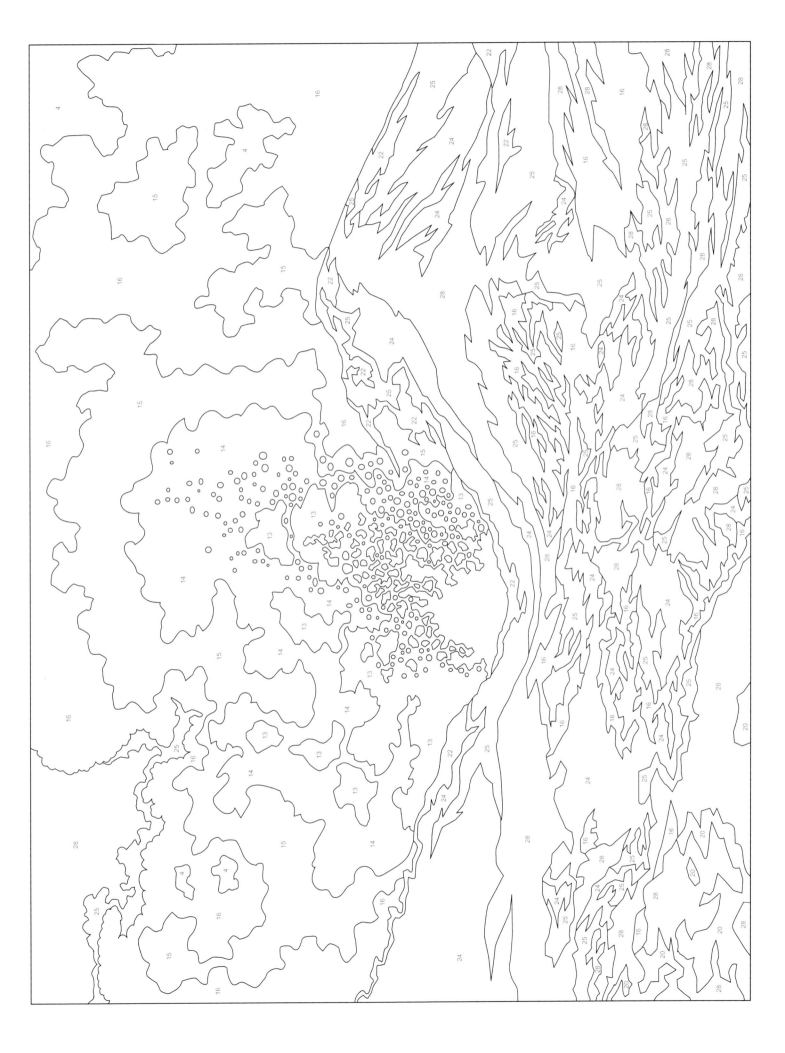

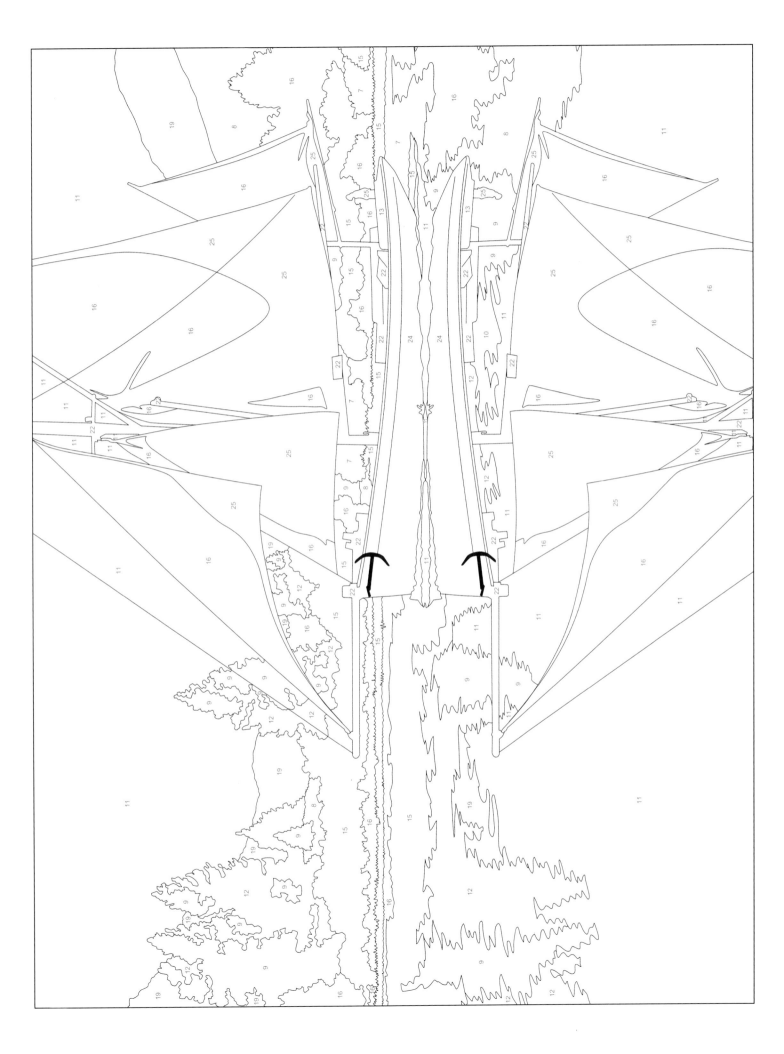